Saving the Planet

Nancy Fornasiero

Series Editor • Mark Pearcy

Contents

Taking Care of Our Planet

Are you responsible for chores at home? Do you fold the laundry or put away the dishes?

Do you have jobs in your classroom? Do you and your classmates take turns with tasks? It is easy to keep things in order that way.

Recycling is one way to help reduce waste.

To keep things clean in a household or school, everyone should pitch in. It is no different when it comes to our environment. Earth is our home. Taking care of it is an important duty.

Governments, businesses, scientists, and community leaders work to protect the environment. But the duty is not theirs alone. It is yours, too. Taking care of our planet is everyone's duty.

Waste is a big problem that is affecting our environment. It is important to learn about the different ways we pollute our planet. We can then reduce the amount of waste we **create.**

A scientist tests the water for pollutants.

Land Pollution

When you throw trash away, it needs to go somewhere. Where does it go?

For Your Information

Plastic water bottles are recyclable. Despite this, only 23 percent of them get recycled. That means 8 out of 10 bottles go to landfills.

Landfills

The waste from our homes usually ends up in landfills. Things that are biodegradable break down. They become soil over time. That is what happens to an apple core that you throw away. Now imagine throwing away an old cell phone. It is not biodegradable. It will never become soil.

Some trash has dangerous chemicals in it. This type of trash is harmful to the environment. It is sometimes known as hazardous waste. This waste can sink into the ground or a nearby water supply. Drinking this water can make people sick.

Biodegradable

Not biodegradable

Landfills get full because most of the trash in them is not biodegradable. But we can reduce the amount of trash we create. We can fix things that are broken. We can reuse things instead of throwing them away. We can also compost things that are biodegradable. These actions will prevent landfills from getting filled up.

Composting

When we compost plants, they break down and become an important part of the soil. Plant materials can break down in a few weeks as long as they are kept warm and moist. The compost can be used as fertilizer in a home garden.

Farming

Land can also become polluted from farming. Some farmers spray chemicals on their crops. The chemicals protect the crops from weeds, insects, and diseases. But some chemicals can cause harm if they enter the soil. They can get into the fruit of a plant.

Too much farming can also be damaging. Using land too often can destroy the nutrients in the soil. Plants need these nutrients for food. To stop this, many farmers leave parts of their land unused for a period of time. This gives the soil time to recover some of the lost nutrients. This can also help prevent diseases that affect plants. These diseases need crops in order to spread. They cannot grow if there are no crops to be found.

Special equipment is used to spray pesticides on crops.

Air Pollution

Earth is surrounded by a layer of air. This layer is called the atmosphere. Pollution harms the atmosphere. Breathing in polluted air is not healthy. Air pollution harms crops, too. Protecting the atmosphere is very important for these reasons.

The Ozone Layer

The ozone layer is part of Earth's atmosphere. Ozone is a special kind of gas. It protects us from harmful rays from the sun. In large doses, these rays can make us very sick.

Sometimes, human-made chemicals can get into the atmosphere. These chemicals make the ozone layer thinner in some places.

Emissions

Cars, planes, trains, and factories release smoke. These **emissions** are caused by the burning of fossil fuels. Coal, oil, and gas are fossil fuels.

Burning fossil fuels releases gases into the air. These gases can mix with the water droplets in clouds. This pollutes the water droplets. The droplets then fall down as acid rain. Acid rain is very harmful.

Fossil fuels are sources of energy from the ground.

Car emissions help create smog in cities.

There are many ways to reduce emissions. People can take public transportation instead of driving. They can also carpool with friends. Some cars run on electricity. These cars produce fewer emissions. Factories can reduce emissions by switching to wind and solar energy. These are clean power sources.

For Your Information

Each year, the United States uses more than 17 million barrels of oil to make plastic bottles. That is enough oil to run a million cars for a year.

Clean Energy Sources

There are many energy sources that do not create pollution.

Solar panels turn the sun's rays into electricity. Wind turbines use the power of the wind to create electricity. The power from the flow of water in rivers can be turned into electricity. This is called hydroelectric power. Energy can even come from under the ground. Heat beneath Earth's surface can be used to warm up cold water. The heated water turns into steam. The steam is used to drive electric generators.

Many countries are using clean energy sources in an effort to help the environment.

Wind turbines

Solar panels

Water Pollution

When waste is dumped into water, the water becomes polluted. This waste can come from factories. It can even come from our homes. Dirty water can make us sick. Many lakes and rivers in the United States are too polluted for use. Many streams and coastlines are polluted, too.

More than one trillion gallons of untreated waste are dumped into our water every year.

Trash is dangerous to sea life.

Factories

Sometimes, factories pour waste right into rivers and streams. This is a **major** source of water pollution. Some factories send their wastewater to a treatment plant. Treatment plants remove harmful chemicals. All the harmful chemicals need to be removed before the water is safe. This treated water then flows into rivers, streams, or the ocean.

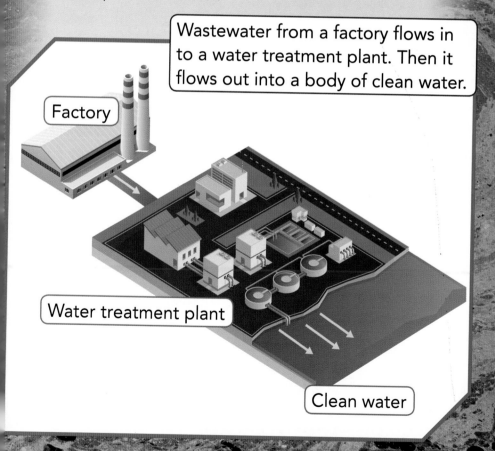

Wastewater from a factory flows in to a water treatment plant. Then it flows out into a body of clean water.

Factory

Water treatment plant

Clean water

Ships

Ships can also pollute water. Some cruise liners dump waste right into the ocean. A shipwreck can release pollutants into the water long after the ship has sunk.

Trash in Our Oceans

In the North Pacific Ocean, water flows clockwise in a huge spiral. This movement of water is called a gyre. A lot of trash collects in the gyre. The trash in the gyre is harmful to sea creatures.

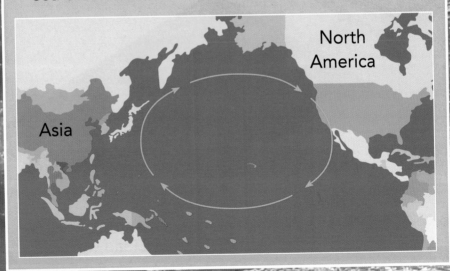

North America

Asia

Our Homes

Your home also creates wastewater. Think about all the dirty water that goes down the drain in your home. All this is wastewater.

In some countries, such as the United States, wastewater is treated. It is cleaned and put back into lakes and rivers. In some countries, wastewater is not treated. Untreated wastewater causes serious pollution. It can make people and animals very sick. It can harm plants, too.

Water treatment plant

What Can You Do?

Pollution from waste is a big problem. It is harming our environment. But this problem can be solved. Choices you make every day can help reduce pollution. Here are a few simple things you can do to help.

Ride your bicycle instead of riding in a car.

Choose products that do not harm the environment.

Use a reusable water bottle.

Use reusable dishes and cups.

Fix things instead of buying new things.

Donate your old toys instead of throwing them out.

Protecting the Environment

You may not realize it, but your actions may be harming the environment. You can act to protect the environment. How will you act to reduce waste today?

Glossary

create: to make

emission: a substance that is sent out into the air

major: main; big

Index